THE COOK'S COLLECTION
❁

DELICIOUS
MEATS

Author: Annette Wolter
Photography: Odette Teubner,
Translated by UPS Translations, London
Edited by Josephine Bacon

CLB 4155
This edition published in 1995 by Grange Books
an imprint of Grange Books PLC, The Grange, Grange Yard, London SE1 3AG
This material published originally under the series title "Kochen Wie Noch Nie"
by Gräfe und Unzer Verlag GmbH, München
© 1995 Gräfe und Unzer Verlag GmbH, München
English translation copyright: © 1995 by CLB Publishing, Godalming, Surrey
Typeset by Image Setting, Brighton, E. Sussex
Printed and bound in Singapore
All rights reserved
ISBN 1-85627-750-X

THE COOK'S COLLECTION

※

DELICIOUS MEATS

Annette Wolter

Grange
BOOKS

Introduction

With today's wide variety of cuts of beef, veal, lamb and pork, at butchers' shops and in supermarkets, available in conveniently prepared portions, there is little excuse not to experiment with all sorts of different meat dishes. The quality of meat has improved over the years, and the price has come down due to intensive farming methods. Recently, however, there has been an upsurge in demand for traditionally farmed meat, and a leaning away from factory farming. Traditionally farmed meat is naturally more expensive, but it is also substantially superior in taste and texture. Many people feel the extra cost to be worthwhile, especially if they only eat meat occasionally. The ethical aspects of choosing traditionally farmed meat is also worth bearing in mind.

The secret to buying meat is to choose the right cut for the recipe. The quicker the meat is to be cooked, the more expensive and therefore tender a cut of meat you will require. A cheaper cut is fine for long, slow casseroling, and it would be a waste to buy fillet steak for such a recipe.

There are some people who hate the sights and smells of the butcher's shop and prefer to buy meat in a supermarket. However, it should be remembered that the butcher is an experienced professional who is only too willing to give you valuable advice on which cut of meat to choose, and will help you with the initial preparation – such as with trimming, cutting, rolling and trussing.

Enjoy adding variety to your everyday meals, as well as your festive menus, with this wonderful array of delicious recipes. The more you try different techniques, the more confident in your meat cookery you will become.

Each recipe serves four, unless otherwise indicated

Steak au Poivre Flambé

Serves 2:
2 x 200g/7oz fillet steaks
1 small onion
1 tbsp black peppercorns
2 tbsps olive oil
Salt
4 tbsps brandy
15g/½oz butter

Preparation time:
20 minutes
Nutritional value:
•1700kJ/400kcal per serving
• 39g protein
• 21g fat
• 4g carbohydrate

Trim the steaks, rinse and pat dry. Tie trussing thread horizontally around the steaks so that the edges are no thinner than the centre. This will ensure that the steaks cook evenly. • Peel and chop the onion. Crush the peppercorns in a mortar with a pestle. • Brush both sides of the steaks with the oil, and dip in the crushed peppercorns. • Heat the remaining oil, and fry the steaks over a high heat for 2-3 minutes. Lower the heat, add the onion and fry until soft. Turn the steaks, and fry for a further 2-3 minutes, then sprinkle with salt. • Gently heat the brandy in a metal ladle over a flame. Pour the warm brandy over the steaks, ignite and gently shake the pan until the flames die down. • Place half the butter on each steak and leave to melt. Turn the steaks once more and transfer to two individual plates, together with the butter and meat juices. Remove the trussing thread. • Serve with garlic bread and a lettuce heart salad.

Tournedos with Sherry Sauce

25g/1oz butter
4 x 150g/5oz tournedos steaks
Salt and freshly ground black pepper
Pinch of hot paprika
3 egg yolks
250ml/8 fl oz beef stock
125ml/4 fl oz dry sherry
1 tbsp lemon juice

Preparation time:
30 minutes
Nutritional value:
Analysis per serving, approx:
• 2400kJ/570kcal
• 47g protein
• 37g fat
• 1g carbohydrate

Melt the butter, and fry the tournedos for 4 minutes, turning frequently. Season lightly with salt and pepper.

Transfer to a plate, cover and keep warm in a preheated oven at its lowest setting. • Beat a little salt and pepper and the paprika into the egg yolks. Place in a hot bain-marie or in a heatproof bowl set over a pan of hot water, and beat until frothy. Mix together the stock and sherry. Beat the stock mixture into the egg yolks in a steady trickle. Continue beating until creamy. Add the lemon juice. Arrange the tournedos on four individual plates, and pour over the sherry sauce. • Serve with roast potatoes and a chicory salad.

Herby Sirloin Slices

2 large marrow-bones
750g/1lb 10oz sirloin steak
40g/1½oz butter
Salt and freshly ground black
pepper
Pinch of grated nutmeg
3 garlic cloves
6 tbsps finely chopped fresh
parsley
3 tbsps finely chopped fresh
basil
7 tbsps breadcrumbs

Preparation time:
50 minutes
Nutritional value:
Analysis per serving, approx:
• 2000kJ/480kcal
• 44g protein
• 28g fat
• 14g carbohydrate

R emove the marrow from
the bones, and dice. •

Rinse the steak and pat dry.
Melt the butter, and fry the
steak over a high heat for 2
minutes on each side. Lower
the heat, and cook for a
further 8-10 minutes on each
side. Season to taste with salt
and pepper, and sprinkle over
the nutmeg. Cover and leave
to rest for 15 minutes. •
Meanwhile, crush the garlic.
Mix together the garlic,
parsley, basil, breadcrumbs and
marrow. Season to taste with
salt and pepper. Coat the steak
with the herb and bone
marrow mixture. • Place the
steak on a baking sheet and
cook in a preheated oven at
240°C/475°F/gas mark 9 until
the crust is golden brown. •
Cut the steak into slices, and
transfer to a serving dish. Serve
with new potatoes and peas or
French beans.

Châteaubriand with Grapefruit Sauce

2 pink grapefruit
150g/5oz softened butter
1 tbsp soy sauce
Pinch of cayenne pepper
Salt and freshly ground white pepper
2 tbsps sunflower oil
750g/1lb 10oz fillet of beef
3 tbsps cress

Preparation time:
45 minutes
Cooking time:
30 minutes
Nutritional value:
Analysis per serving, approx:
• 1300kJ/310kcal
• 37g protein
• 14g fat
• 12g carbohydrate

Halve 1 grapefruit and squeeze out the juice. Peel the other grapefruit, remove the pith and separate into segments. Set aside in the refrigerator. • Mix together the grapefruit juice, butter, soy sauce and cayenne pepper, and season to taste with salt and pepper. Chill in the refrigerator for at least 30 minutes. • Heat the oil in a flameproof casserole, and fry the steak over a high heat for 2 minutes on each side. Cover and transfer the casserole to a preheated oven at 180°C/350°F/gas mark 4, and cook for a further 25 minutes. • Season to taste with salt and pepper, wrap in aluminium foil and keep warm in a cool oven. • Drain the meat juices from the casserole and discard. Melt the butter and grapefruit juice mixture in the casserole over a low heat. Reduce by a third, and season to taste with salt and pepper. • Add the grapefruit segments and heat through. Sprinkle the cress over the sauce. • Cut the meat into slices and arrange on a serving dish. Spoon over the sauce. • Serve with tagliatelle.

10

Budapest Goulash

800g/1lb 12oz boneless fore rib of beef
500g/1lb 2oz onions
2 garlic cloves
50g/2oz streaky bacon, rinded
25g/1oz lard
3 tbsps paprika
½ tsp ground caraway seeds
½ tsp dried marjoram
2 tbsps tomato purée
250ml/8 fl oz hot beef stock
Salt
250g/8oz floury potatoes
1 green pepper
1 red pepper

Preparation time:
15 minutes
Cooking time:
1 hour
Nutritional value:
Analysis per serving, approx:
• 2900kJ/690kcal
• 43g protein
• 47g fat
• 25g carbohydrate

Rinse the meat, pat dry and cut into 2cm/1inch cubes. • Peel and finely chop the onions and garlic. Dice the bacon. • Melt the lard, and fry the bacon. Add the onions and garlic, and fry until soft. • Add the meat to the pan, increase the heat and fry, stirring frequently, until brown on all sides. • Remove the pan from the heat, and add the paprika, caraway seeds, dried marjoram, tomato purée and 125ml/4 fl oz of the stock, and season to taste with salt. Return to the heat, cover and simmer for 30 minutes. • Peel and dice the potatoes. Halve, seed, wash and dice the peppers. • Add the potatoes and the remaining stock to the goulash, and cook for a further 15 minutes. • Add the peppers and cook for a further 15 minutes. Serve immediately.

One-pot Hungarian Goulash

Serves 8:

1kg/2¼lbs chuck steak
350g/11oz onions
250g/8oz carrots
200g/7oz baby turnips
1 head celery
40g/1½oz lard
3 tbsps sweet paprika
750ml/1¼pints hot beef stock
750g/1lb 10oz floury potatoes
1 tsp caraway seeds
Salt

Preparation time:
40 minutes
Cooking time:
1¼ hours
Nutritional value:
Analysis per serving, approx:
• 1400kJ/330kcal
• 30g protein
• 13g fat
• 25g carbohydrate

Rinse the meat, pat dry and cut into 2cm/1inch cubes. • Peel and chop the onions. Peel the carrots and turnips. Trim and wash the celery. Cut the carrots into matchstick strips. Thinly slice the turnips. Dice the celery. • Melt the lard, and fry the onions until soft. Add the meat and fry, stirring frequently, until browned on all sides. • Remove the pan from the heat and sprinkle over the paprika. Add the carrots, turnips, celery and stock. Return the pan to the heat, cover and simmer for 45 minutes. • Peel and dice the potatoes. Add the potatoes and caraway seeds to the pan, and season to taste with salt. Cook for a further 30 minutes until the meat is tender. Serve immediately.

Oxtail Stew

1.25kg/2¾lbs oxtail, chopped
into 5cm/2inch pieces
500g/1lb 2oz onions
2 garlic cloves
100g/4oz carrots
100g/4oz celery sticks
4 tbsps olive oil
500ml/16 fl oz dry red wine
1 tbsp meat stock granules
½ tsp caraway seeds
½ tsp dried thyme
2 bay leaves
Salt and freshly ground black
pepper
50g/2oz coarsely ground rye
flour
100ml/3 fl oz double cream
2 tbsps finely chopped fresh
parsley

Preparation time:
30 minutes
Cooking time:
2½ hours
Nutritional value:
Analysis per serving, approx:
• 3900kJ/930kcal
• 68g protein
• 52g fat
• 24g carbohydrate

Rinse the meat and pat dry.
Peel and chop the
onions and garlic. Peel and
finely chop the carrots. Trim,
wash and chop the celery. •
Heat the oil, and fry the oxtail
over high heat, stirring
frequently, until browned on
all sides. Add the onions,
garlic, carrots and celery, and
continue to cook until the
onions are soft. • Add the
wine, stock granules, caraway
seeds, thyme and bay leaves,
and season to taste with salt
and pepper. Cover and simmer
for 2 hours. • Remove the
oxtail from the pan, and strain
and reserve the cooking liquid.
Cut the meat from the bones.
• Mix together the flour and
cream. If necessary, add a little
water to make a smooth paste.
Stir the paste into the reserved
cooking liquid. Bring to the
boil in a clean pan and simmer
gently for 5 minutes. • Return
the meat to the saucepan to
heat. Adjust the seasoning and
transfer to a serving dish.
Sprinkle over the parsley. •
Serve with broccoli au gratin.

Special Steak and Kidney Pie

Serves 6:

500g/1lb 2oz calves' kidneys
500g/1lb 2oz beef fillet
1 medium onion
3 tbsps flour
Salt and freshly ground black pepper
2 tbsps shredded beef suet or 25g/1oz lard
125ml/4 fl oz water
6 tbsps dry sherry
½ tsp Worcestershire sauce
3 tbsps finely chopped fresh parsley
150g/5oz frozen puff pastry dough, thawed
1 egg yolk
1 tbsp milk

Soak for 1 hour
Preparation time:
45 minutes
Bake for 1 hour
Nutritional value:
Analysis per serving, approx:
• 1800kJ/430kcal
• 35g protein
• 24g fat
• 15g carbohydrate

Trim, halve and core the kidneys. Place in a bowl, cover with cold water and leave to soak for 1 hour. Change the water several times. • Rinse the kidneys, pat dry and cut into cubes. • Rinse the beef, pat dry and cut into cubes the same size. • Peel and finely chop the onion. • Season the flour with salt and pepper. Coat the beef and kidneys in the seasoned flour. • Melt the suet or lard in a large frying pan, and fry the onion until soft. Add the meat and fry, stirring frequently, until brown on all sides. Remove from the heat and transfer to a large pie dish or shallow, ovenproof dish. • Mix together the water, sherry, Worcestershire sauce and parsley, and heat gently. Pour the sherry mixture over the meat. • Roll out the dough on a lightly floured surface into a sheet slightly larger than the dish. Brush the rim of the pie dish, if using, with a little water, cut a strip of dough and press firmly in position on the

rim. Brush with a little water, and place the remaining dough over the filling. Press the edges firmly together to seal. Trim the overlap and knock up the edges. • If you are using a dish that does not have a flat rim, roll out the dough as above, and place the entire sheet over the dish. It should overlap the edge of the dish by about 2cm/1inch to prevent the filling bubbling out during cooking. Press the overlapping pastry firmly against the edge of the dish. • Make a small hole in the middle of the pie to allow the steam to escape. • Roll out the trimmings, and cut out decorative shapes with a pastry cutter or sharp knife. • Beat together the egg yolk and milk, and lightly brush over the surface of the pie. Arrange the pastry shapes on top, and brush with the egg and milk glaze. • Bake the pie in a preheated oven at 220°C/ 425°F/gas mark 7 for 30 minutes. Lower the temperature to 180°C/350°F/

gas mark 4, and bake for a further 30 minutes. • Serve the pie straight from the dish with a chicory or oak leaf lettuce salad.

Our tip: *If you do not have a suitable pie dish, use a large cake tin. It may then be necessary to thaw more pastry to line the base and sides of the tin to prevent the meat from acquiring a metallic taste.*

Chateaubriand en Croûte

50g/2oz horseradish
100g/4oz unsalted butter
150g/5oz mushrooms
600g/1lb 6oz fillet of beef
*Salt and freshly ground white
pepper*
25g/1oz butter
*300g/10oz frozen puff pastry
dough, thawed*
*100g/4oz cooked ham, thinly
sliced*
1 egg
1 tbsp cream
1 egg yolk

Preparation time:
40 minutes
Cooking time:
25 minutes
Nutritional value:
Analysis per serving, approx:
- 3800kJ/900kcal
- 46g protein
- 68g fat
- 27g carbohydrate

Peel and finely grate the horseradish. Cream the butter and beat in the horseradish. Set aside. • Thinly slice the mushrooms. • Trim the beef, rinse and pat dry. Flatten the beef to 3cm/1inch thick. Rub in a little salt and pepper. Melt the butter over a high heat, and fry the beef for 2 minutes on each side. Remove from the pan and cool. • Fry the mushrooms in the same pan for 2 minutes. Season then remove from the pan. • Halve the pastry. Roll out on a lightly floured surface to 2 ovals slightly longer and wider than the beef. Reserve the trimmings. • Rinse a baking sheet in cold water. Transfer 1 pastry oval to the baking sheet, and cover with the ham. Spoon over half the mushrooms, place the beef on top and cover with mushrooms. • Beat the egg and cream. Brush the edges of the dough with the egg and cream mixture. Carefully lift the remaining dough oval and place it over the beef. Press the edges firmly together to seal. • Cut a hole in the top to allow the steam to escape. Brush the top of the dough with the egg and cream. Decorate with the trimmings and brush with egg and cream. • Cook in a

preheated oven at 220°C/
450°F/gas mark 7 for 12
minutes. Switch off the oven,
and leave to rest for 10
minutes before serving. • Mix
the egg yolk and flavoured
butter, warm through and
serve separately.

Braised Beef

1 x 800g/1lb 12oz rump of
beef
2 carrots
2 onions
50g/2oz unsmoked streaky
bacon, rinded
4 white peppercorns
Parsley sprig
Salt and freshly ground white
pepper
15g/1oz butter
1 tbsp flour
2 tbsps tomato purée
½ tsp English mustard
½ tsp sugar
6 tbsps soured cream

Preparation time:
30 minutes
Cooking time:
1½ hours
Nutritional value:
Analysis per serving, approx:
• 2100kJ/500kcal
• 46g protein
• 26g fat
• 17g carbohydrate

Trim the beef, if necessary.
• Peel and chop the carrots
and onions. Dice the bacon. •
Fry the bacon in a dry pan
until the fat runs. Add the
beef, and fry until browned on
all sides. Add the carrots,
onions, peppercorns and
parsley, and season to taste
with salt. Gently fry for 10
minutes, stirring frequently. •
Bring 200ml/7 fl oz water to
the boil, and pour into the
pan, cover and cook over a
low heat for 1 hour. From
time to time, add more hot
water to prevent the beef from
drying out. • Remove the beef
from the pan and keep warm. •
Strain and measure the braising
liquid. Make up to 375ml/14
fl oz with hot water. • Melt
the butter, and stir in the flour.
Cook, stirring constantly, for 2
minutes until lightly browned.
Stir in the tomato purée.
Gradually stir in the strained
braising liquid. Season with
pepper, and stir in the mustard,
sugar and soured cream. •
Carve the braised beef, arrange
on a serving dish and pour
over a little sauce. Hand the
remaining sauce separately.
Serve with mashed potato and
red cabbage.

Beef with Caramelized Onions

500g/1lb 2oz onions
1 tsp sugar
Salt and freshly ground white
pepper
25g/1oz butter
4 x 150g/5oz slices silverside
2 tsps flour
2 tbsps vegetable oil
250ml/8 fl oz beef stock
6 tbsps dry red wine

Preparation time:
50 minutes
Nutritional value:
Analysis per serving, approx:
• 1700kJ/400kcal
• 33g protein
• 24g fat
• 13g carbohydrate

Peel and slice the onions and push out into rings. Mix together the sugar and ½ tsp salt, and sprinkle over the onions. • Melt the butter in a large pan, and very gently fry the onion rings for 40 minutes until golden brown. Set aside. • Rinse the slices of beef and pat dry. Beat with a steak hammer, a wooden rolling pin or the heal of your hand. Rub in a little salt and pepper, and coat with flour. • Heat the oil in a clean pan, and fry the beef over a high heat for 1 minute on each side. Lower the heat, and fry for a further 3 minutes on each side. Remove from the pan, transfer to a serving dish and keep warm. • Add the stock and heat, scraping the base of the pan with a wooden spatula to deglaze. Add the wine, and season to taste with salt and pepper. • Reheat the onion rings, and arrange on top of the beef. Pour over the sauce. • Serve with boiled potatoes and a lamb's lettuce salad.

Fillet of Beef in a Savoy Cabbage Parcel

Serves 6:

25g/1oz butter
1kg/2¼lbs fillet of beef
Salt and freshly ground white pepper
175g/6oz sausagemeat
2 tbsps finely chopped fresh parsley
1 tsp dried thyme
10 large Savoy cabbage leaves
125ml/4 fl oz beef stock
200ml/6 fl oz double cream
1 tsp cornflour

Preparation time:
40 minutes
Cooking time:
40 minutes
Nutritional value:
Analysis per serving, approx:
• 2400kJ/570kcal
• 40g protein
• 42g fat
• 6g carbohydrate

Melt the butter and brown the beef on all sides. Rub in a little salt and pepper, cover and leave to rest. • Mix together the sausagemeat, parsley and thyme. • Blanch the Savoy cabbage leaves in boiling water for 5 minutes. Drain and trim the main stalks. Arrange the leaves in a rectangle large enough to enclose the beef. Coat the leaves with the sausagemeat mixture. • Wrap the fillet in the leaves and tie with trussing thread. • Place the beef parcel inside a roasting bag, and add the stock. Seal the bag and prick the top with a needle several times. • Cook in a preheated oven at 220° C/450° F/gas mark 7 for 15 minutes. Reduce the temperature to 180°C/350°F/ gas mark 4, and cook for a further 15 minutes. • Transfer the beef to a carving dish. Pour the cooking juices into a saucepan and set over a low heat. Mix together the cream and cornflour to make a smooth paste. Stir the cornflour paste into the sauce and cook, stirring, until thickened. • Serve the beef and sauce separately.

Meatballs
with Radish Vinaigrette

1 thick slice day-old bread,
crusts removed
3 spring onions
1 small yellow pepper
65g/2½oz butter
600g/1lb 6oz minced beef
1 egg, lightly beaten
1 egg yolk
½ tsp sweet paprika
1 tsp Worcestershire sauce
Salt and freshly ground pepper
8 tbsps sunflower oil
6 tbsps white wine vinegar
2 bunches radishes
3 tbsps snipped fresh chives

Preparation time:
1 hour
Nutritional value:
Analysis per serving, approx:
• 3400kJ/810kcal
• 40g protein
• 66g fat
• 15g carbohydrate

Tear the bread into small
pieces, place in a bowl and
cover with water. Leave to
soak. • Trim the spring onions
and cut into thin rings. Halve,
seed, wash and dice the
pepper. • Melt 25g/1oz of the
butter, and fry the onions for 3
minutes. Add the pepper, and
fry for a further 3 minutes. •
Squeeze the water from the
bread, and mix with the
minced beef, onions and
pepper, egg, egg yolk, paprika
and Worcestershire sauce.
Season to taste with salt and
pepper. Knead the mixture
thoroughly. • Break off small
pieces of the mixture, and
shape into balls about the size
of a walnut. Melt the
remaining butter, and fry the
meatballs until golden brown
all over. Remove from the pan
with a slotted spoon and leave
to cool. • Gradually beat the
oil into the vinegar. • Trim
and finely chop the radishes.
Mix the radishes and chives
into the vinaigrette, and season
to taste with salt and pepper. •
Serve the meatballs with the
vinaigrette and wholemeal
rolls.

Holstein Schnitzel

4 thin slices smoked salmon
8 pickled gherkins
4 x 150g/5oz veal escalopes
40g/1½oz butter
Salt and freshly ground white
pepper
4 eggs
2 tbsps capers
2 thick slices bread, toasted and
cut into triangles
4 canned anchovy fillets,
drained
2 tsps black lumpfish roe
225g/8oz sliced pickled
beetroot
2 tbsps finely chopped fresh
parsley

Preparation time:
45 minutes
Nutritional value:
Analysis per serving, approx:
• 2300kJ/550kcal
• 54g protein
• 29g fat
• 19g carbohydrate

Roll up the salmon slices into cornets. Make several lengthways cuts in the gherkins to create fans. • Rinse the veal and pat dry. • Melt the butter in a frying pan. Fry the escalopes for 4 minutes on each side. Season with salt and pepper to taste. Keep warm in a preheated oven at the lowest setting. • Fry the eggs in the same pan until the yolks have just set. Sprinkle with salt. • Arrange the veal on four plates and top each escalope with a fried egg. Sprinkle over the capers. Surround the meat with the toast triangles, salmon cornets, gherkins, anchovy fillets, roe and beetroot. Garnish with parsley and serve immediately.

Calves Liver in White Wine Butter

4 shallots
75g/3oz button mushrooms
175g/6oz butter
375ml/14 fl oz dry white wine
Salt and freshly ground white pepper
1 tbsp finely chopped fresh tarragon or 1 tsp dried tarragon
600g/1lb 6oz calves' liver, cut into in 2cm/1inch thick slices

Preparation time:
50 minutes
Nutritional value:
Analysis per serving, approx:
• 2400kJ/570kcal
• 28g protein
• 42g fat
• 11g carbohydrate

Peel and finely chop the shallots. Thinly slice the mushrooms. • Dice 100g/4oz of the butter and chill in the refrigerator. Melt 25g/1oz of the remaining butter, and fry the shallots until soft. Add the white wine, and boil until reduced by a third. • Vigorously whisk the diced butter into the wine, one piece at a time, until thick and creamy. Season to taste with salt and pepper. • Add the mushrooms, and cook over a low heat for 5 minutes. Sprinkle over the tarragon and keep the sauce warm. • Rinse the liver and pat dry. Melt the remaining butter, and fry the liver for 1 minute on each side. Season to taste with salt and pepper and serve with the white wine and butter sauce. • Potato cakes make an excellent accompaniment.

Veal Cordon Bleu

4 x 200g/7oz veal escalopes
Salt and freshly ground white pepper
4 thin slices cooked ham
4 thin slices Emmenthal cheese
1 tsp sweet paprika
2 eggs
4 tbsps flour
6 tbsps breadcrumbs
3 tbsps sunflower oil
25g/1oz butter
½ lemon, cut into wedges
4 parsley sprigs (optional)

Preparation time:
30 minutes
Nutritional value:
Analysis per serving, approx:
• 2700kJ/640kcal
• 59g protein
• 37g fat
• 19g carbohydrate

Rinse, trim and beat the escalopes until thin. Rub salt and pepper to taste into both sides. • Place 1 slice of ham on half of each escalope, and top each with 1 slice of cheese. Sprinkle over a little paprika. Fold each escalope over the filing and secure with cocktail sticks. • Place the eggs, flour and breadcrumbs in three separate bowls. Lightly beat the eggs. Heat the oil and butter in a frying pan. • Dip the veal first in the flour, then in the beaten eggs and finally in the breadcrumbs. • Fry the escalopes for 6 minutes on each side. • Transfer to four individual plates and remove the cocktail sticks. Garnish with lemon wedges and parsley, if using. • Serve with French beans, grilled tomatoes and potato croquettes.

Our tip: *Instead of using the larger veal escalopes, which you need to beat thin, you may be able to buy butterfly slices. These are smaller but thicker slices, which have been cut open and flattened.*

Veal Fricassée French Style

750g/1lb 10oz shoulder of veal
250g/8oz small shallots
1 onion
1 carrot
1 celery stick
250g/8oz mushrooms
5 parsley sprigs
1 thyme sprig
3 cloves
50g/2oz butter
1 bay leaf
250ml/8 fl oz dry white wine
125ml/4 fl oz water
Salt and freshly ground white pepper
2 egg yolks
125ml/4 fl oz single cream
Juice of 1 lemon
Pinch of grated nutmeg
1 tsp cornflour

Preparation time:
30 minutes
Cooking time:
1¼ hours
Nutritional value:
Analysis per serving, approx:
• 2900kJ/690kcal
• 52g protein
• 40g fat
• 19g carbohydrate

Trim any excess fat or skin from the meat. Rinse and cut into 3cm/1inch cubes. • Peel the shallots, onion and carrot. Rinse the celery and cut into 4 pieces. Wipe the mushrooms and cut in half. • Rinse the parsley and thyme. Stud the onion with the cloves. • Melt the butter, and fry the meat and the shallots until tender but not brown. Place the onion, carrot, celery, parsley, thyme, bay leaf, wine and water in a saucepan, and season to taste with salt and pepper. Bring to the boil, cover and simmer for 1 hour. • Strain the vegetable stock and discard the vegetables and herbs. Transfer to a clean pan, and add the mushrooms. Simmer for 15 minutes. • Beat together the egg yolks, cream, lemon juice, nutmeg and cornflour, and then stir into the fricassée. • Transfer to a serving dish and serve with buttered tagliatelle.

Lamb Pâté with Sweetbreads

Serves 12:
500g/1lb 2oz boneless saddle
of lamb
100g/4oz white bread, crusts
removed
Pinch of dried mint
Pinch of dried rosemary
Salt and freshly ground white
pepper
1 egg white
250ml/8 fl oz whipping cream
400g/14oz lambs' or calves'
sweetbreads
50g/2oz canned or bottled
truffles
1 tbsp finely chopped fresh
basil
500g/1lb 2oz flour
175g/6oz chilled butter, diced
1 egg, lightly beaten
1 tbsp iced water
1 egg yolk, lightly beaten

Preparation time:
1½ hours
Leave to cool for 12 hours
Cooking time:
1 hour

Nutritional value:
Analysis per serving, approx:
• 1900kJ/450kcal
• 23g protein
• 25g fat
• 37g carbohydrate

Trim the lamb, rinse and
pat dry. Cut the meat into
thin slices and place on a dish.
• Thinly slice the bread, and
place on top of the meat. •
Mix together the mint,
rosemary and a pinch of salt
and pepper. Sprinkle the herb
mixture over the bread. •
Whisk together the egg white
and 6 tbsps of the cream, and
pour over the bread. Cover
and leave in the refrigerator for
12 hours. • Meanwhile, soak
the sweetbreads in cold water
for at least 5 hours, changing
the water several times. •
When the sweetbreads have
become white and the water
remains clear, drain them.
Bring a pan of lightly salted
water to the boil. Add the
sweetbreads, and simmer for

10 minutes. Drain and refresh in cold water. • Trim and chop the sweetbreads, and set aside. • Whisk the remaining cream until stiff. • Pass the lamb and bread mixture through a mincer on the finest setting. Set the mixing bowl over a bowl of ice cubes, and stir the whipped cream into the minced lamb mixture. • Drain and dice the truffles, and reserve the juice. Stir the truffles, truffle juice, basil and sweetbreads into the minced lamb mixture. Place the bowl in the refrigerator. • Sift the flour into a mixing bowl. Add the butter, and rub it into the flour with the fingertips until the mixture resembles fine breadcrumbs. Make a well in the centre, and add the egg and iced water. Gradually incorporate the dry ingredients with the fingertips, and knead lightly. Turn the dough out onto a lightly floured surface, and knead again. • Divide the dough in half, and roll out to two 30cm/12inch circles. •

Line a 26cm/10inch springform tin with 1 dough circle, easing it gently to fit. Prick the dough all over with a fork. • Spoon the minced lamb mixture into the dough case, and smooth the top. Brush the edge of the remaining dough circle with the egg yolk, and lift it over the filling. Press the edges together firmly to seal. Trim off any excess dough, and reserve. • Prick the top with a fork to allow the steam to escape during cooking. Brush the top with beaten egg yolk. Roll out the dough trimmings, and cut out small decorative shapes. Brush these with egg yolk and place on top of the pie. Brush again with egg yolk. • Bake in a preheated oven at 220°C/425°F/gas mark 7 for 1 hour. If necessary, cover the pie with baking parchment or foil to prevent the top burning. • Transfer the pie in the tin to a cooling rack for 15 minutes. Remove from the tin and allow to cool completely.

Lamb Cutlets with Cracked Wheat

1 onion
500g/1lb 2oz French beans
2 tbsps olive oil
50g/2oz cracked wheat
375ml/14 fl oz water
½ tsp vegetable stock granules
1/2 tsp dried savory
1 tbsp finely chopped fresh
basil or ½ tsp dried basil
Salt and freshly ground black
pepper
4 x 150g/5oz lamb cutlets
2 tbsps grapeseed oil
4 tbsps dry red wine
1 beef tomato, cut into wedges

Preparation time:
15 minutes
Cooking time:
30 minutes
Nutritional value:
Analysis per serving, approx:
• 3100kJ/740kcal
• 28g protein
• 58g fat
• 22g carbohydrate

Peel and chop the onion. •
Rinse, trim and halve the
French beans. • Heat the olive
oil, and gently fry the onion
and cracked wheat, stirring
frequently, until the onion is
soft. • Bring the water to the
boil, and add the vegetable
stock granules, savory, basil
and a pinch of pepper. Add the
beans and cook for 25 minutes.
• Rinse the cutlets and pat dry,
Make cuts across the fatty rind
every 5cm/2inches. Rub in a
little pepper. • Heat the
grapeseed oil, and fry the
cutlets over a medium heat for
3-4 minutes on each side. •
Drain the beans and mix with
the onion and cracked wheat.
Transfer the lamb cutlets to a
serving dish and arrange the
beans beside them. Season
lightly with salt. • Add the red
wine to the pan, heat, scraping
the base of the pan with a
wooden spatula to deglaze.
Pour the red wine sauce over
the lamb. Garnish with tomato
wedges and serve.

Lamb Cutlets with Avocado and Garlic Cream

1 ripe avocado pear
Salt and freshly ground white
pepper
4 garlic cloves
125ml/4 fl oz whipping cream
2 tbsps finely chopped fresh
basil
4 x 150g/5oz lamb cutlets
40g/1½oz butter
1 tbsp flour

Preparation time:
30 minutes
Nutritional value:
Analysis per serving, approx:
• 3600kJ/860kcal
• 25g protein
• 81g fat
• 7g carbohydrate

Halve and stone the avocado pear, and scoop out the flesh. Rub the flesh through a fine sieve, and mix with ½ tsp salt. Crush the garlic, and mix with the puréed avocado pear. • Whip the cream until stiff. Fold the cream into the purée. Gently mix in the basil. Chill in the refrigerator. • Rinse the cutlets, pat dry and cut off the fatty rind, exposing about 5cm/ 2inches of the rib bone. • Melt 15g/½oz of the butter. Rub salt and pepper into the cutlets, and dip them first in the melted butter and then in the flour. • Melt the remaining butter in a pan, and fry the cutlets over a high heat for 3 minutes on each side. • Arrange the cutlets on four individual plates, and spoon over the avocado and garlic cream. • Serve with broccoli.

34

Lamb Medallions with Cheesy Tomatoes

8 small, ripe tomatoes
Salt
125ml/4 fl oz hot beef stock
4 x 150g/5oz lamb
medallions
60g/2½oz butter
½ tsp sweet paprika
4 tbsps fine breadcrumbs
8 tsps freshly grated
Emmenthal cheese
4 tbsps sunflower oil

Preparation time:
40 minutes
Nutritional value:
Analysis per serving, approx:
• 2900kJ/690kcal
• 23g protein
• 61g fat
• 13g carbohydrate

Rinse the tomatoes and make 2 deep cuts in the rounded ends of each one. Open up the cuts and sprinkle with a little salt. • Place the tomatoes in a small ovenproof dish, pour in the hot stock and bake in a preheated oven at 230°C/450°F/gas mark 8 for 10 minutes. • Rinse the lamb medallions, pat dry and cut off any fat or skin. Flatten firmly with the heel of your hand. Tie trussing thread horizontally around the medallions. • Melt 25g/1oz of the butter. Rub the paprika into the lamb and season to taste with salt. Dip the lamb first in the melted butter and then in the breadcrumbs. • Remove the tomatoes from the oven, and top each with 1 tsp of cheese and dot with the remaining butter. Return to the oven and bake for a further 10 minutes. • Heat the oil, and fry the lamb over a medium heat for 3 minutes on each side. • Remove the trussing thread. Arrange the cheese-topped tomatoes and the lamb medallions on a serving plate. • Serve with garlic bread.

Lamb Ragoût with Haricot Beans

200g/7oz white haricot beans
1 bouquet garni
750g/1lb 10oz shoulder of
lamb
3 tbsps olive oil
600g/1lb 6oz beef tomatoes
400g/14oz baby onions
Salt and freshly ground pepper
750ml/1¼ pints beef stock
1 rosemary sprig
1 bay leaf
1 clove
2 tbsps balsamic or red wine
vinegar
2 tbsps finely chopped fresh
parsley

Preparation time:
40 minutes, plus soaking time
Cooking time:
1½ hours
Nutritional value:
Analysis per serving, approx:
• 2500kJ/600kcal
• 39 g protein
• 41 g fat
• 20 g carbohydrate

Soak the beans in cold water for 8 hours or overnight. • Transfer the beans and the soaking water to a pan, and bring to the boil. Add the bouquet garni, cover and simmer for 1 hour or until almost cooked. • Rinse the lamb, pat dry and cut into 3cm/1inch cubes. Heat the oil, and fry the lamb in batches. Remove from the heat and set aside. • Skin and coarsely chop the tomatoes. • Peel the onions, and fry in the hot oil until soft. Add the lamb, tomatoes, stock, rosemary, bay leaf and clove, and season to taste with salt and pepper. Bring to the boil, and cook over a medium heat for about 40 minutes. • Drain the beans and discard the bouquet garni. Add the beans to the lamb, and cook for a further 20 minutes. Stir in the vinegar. Transfer the ragoût to a serving dish. Remove and discard the rosemary sprig, bay leaf and clove. Sprinkle over the parsley. • Serve with crusty white bread.

Lamb Ragoût with Rye

400g/14oz leg of lamb
2 onions
2 garlic cloves
4 tbsps olive oil
Salt and freshly ground black
pepper
Pinch of cayenne pepper
50g/2oz coarsely ground rye
flour
250ml/8 fl oz dry red wine
250ml/8 fl oz water
100ml/3½ fl oz single cream
3 tbsps snipped fresh chives

Preparation time:
45 minutes
Nutritional value:
Analysis per serving, approx:
• 2100kJ/500kcal
• 22g protein
• 34g fat
• 6g carbohydrate

Rinse the lamb, pat dry and
cut into 3cm/1inch
chunks. • Peel and chop the
onions and garlic. Heat the oil,
and fry the onions and garlic
until soft. Remove with a
slotted spoon and set aside. •
Sprinkle the lamb with a little
pepper, and fry in the hot oil
for about 5 minutes, stirring
frequently. • Sprinkle over the
cayenne pepper and rye flour,
and season to taste with salt.
Cook for a further 2 minutes. •
Return the onions and garlic
to the pan, and add the wine
and water. Simmer, uncovered,
until the lamb is tender. •
Remove the ragoût from the
heat and stir in the cream and
chives. • Serve with browned
polenta or parsley dumplings.

Stuffed Breast of Lamb

2 onions
2 garlic cloves
1 carrot
4 tbsps olive oil
1 tbsp coarsely ground barley
1 tbsp cracked wheat
1 tbsp coarsely ground oats
1 tbsp coarsely ground rye
125ml/4 fl oz water
Sea salt and freshly ground
black pepper
Pinch of cayenne pepper
1 egg, lightly beaten
2 tbsps finely chopped fresh
mixed herbs
1kg/2¼lbs boned breast of
lamb
250ml/8 fl oz dry red wine
2 tsps vegetable stock granules
6 tbsps cream

Preparation time:
30 minutes
Cooking time:
1¾ hours
Nutritional value:
Analysis per serving, approx:
• 5200kJ/1200kcal
• 37g protein
• 110g fat
• 18g carbohydrate

Peel and finely chop the onions and garlic. • Peel and chop the carrot. • Heat 2 tbsps of the oil, and fry the onions, garlic and carrot until soft. • Stir in the barley, cracked wheat, oats and rye, and fry for 2-3 minutes. Add the water, and season to taste with salt and pepper. Simmer for 5 minutes. Remove from the heat, cover and leave to stand for 10 minutes. • Stir the cayenne pepper, egg and mixed herbs into the mixture. • Rub the lamb with a little pepper. Spread the cereal and herb filling evenly over the breast. Roll up and secure with trussing thread. • Heat the remaining oil in a roasting tin, and fry the lamb until browned on all sides. Add the wine and stock granules. Roast in a preheated oven at 220°C/425°F/gas mark 7 for 1½

hours. • Transfer the lamb to a carving dish, and remove the trussing thread. Cut into slices, and arrange on a serving dish. Stir the cream into the meat juices and serve with the lamb.

Crown Roast

2 x 1kg/2¼lbs racks of lamb
4 garlic cloves
2 shallots
2 tbsps sesame oil
2 tsps chopped fresh thyme
½ tsp dried sage
Salt and ground black pepper
2 tbsps sunflower oil
1 onion
1 carrot
100g/4oz celery sticks
100g/4oz leeks
125ml/4 fl oz dry red wine
125ml/4 fl oz beef stock
150ml/5 fl oz double cream

Marinate for 16 hours
Preparation time:
30 minutes
Cooking time:
40 minutes
Nutritional value:
Analysis per serving, approx:
• 3500kJ/830kcal
• 27g protein
• 76g fat
• 6g carbohydrate

Curve the racks so that their ends touch, and tie securely. • Peel and chop 2 garlic cloves and the shallots. Mix with the oil, thyme, sage and pepper. Coat the crown with the oil, wrap in foil and marinate for 16 hours. • Scrape the oil from the joint, and reserve. • Sprinkle the lamb with salt. Oil a roasting tin. Place the lamb in the tin, and roast in a preheated oven at 220°C/450°F/gas mark 7 for 20 minutes. • Meanwhile, peel and chop the onion, carrot., celery and leeks. Arrange the vegetables around the crown roast. Reserve 25ml/1 fl oz each of wine stock. Spoon the remainder over the meat. Return to the oven for 20 minutes. • Remove the lamb from the tin and set aside. • Add the reserved wine and stock to the juices. Set over a low heat, scrape the tin to deglaze. Strain the sauce. Stir in the marinade and cream. Peel and crush the remaining garlic, and mix in. • Remove the thread, and serve with the sauce.

Leg of Lamb au Gratin

5 garlic cloves
1.5kg/3½lbs leg of lamb
1 tsp finely chopped fresh
thyme
Juice of 1 lemon
4 tbsps sunflower oil
Salt and ground black pepper
750g/1lb 10oz courgettes
2 onions
750g/1lb 10oz floury potatoes
50g/2oz Emmenthal cheese,
grated
125ml/4 fl oz crème fraîche
Bunch of basil

Marinate for 12 hours
Preparation time:
40 minutes
Cooking time:
1½ hours
Nutritional value:
Analysis per serving, approx:
• 3800kJ/900kcal
• 54g protein
• 61g fat
• 33g carbohydrate

Peel and slice 4 garlic cloves into slivers. Make small incisions in the lamb joint and insert the garlic. Place the lamb in a large dish. Mix the thyme, lemon juice and 2 tbsps of the oil, and season to taste with pepper. Pour over the lamb, and marinate for 12 hours. • Trim, rinse and thinly slice the courgettes. Peel and thinly slice the onions and potatoes. • Rub a little salt into the lamb. Heat the remaining oil in a roasting tin, and fry the lamb for 10 minutes until browned on all sides. • Add the courgettes, onions and potatoes. Roast in a preheated oven at 180°C/350°F/gas mark 4 for 1 hour. • Sprinkle the cheese over the lamb, and return to oven for 30 minutes. • Peel the remaining garlic. Place the crème fraîche, garlic clove, basil and salt and pepper to taste in a blender, and work to a purée. Transfer the lamb and vegetables to a serving dish, and hand the basil sauce separately.

Pork Chops with Potatoes and Onions

500g/1lb 2oz floury potatoes
2 onions
25g/1oz lard
Salt and freshly ground black pepper
1 tsp dried thyme
250ml/8 fl oz chicken stock
4 x 175g/6oz pork chops
3 tbsps finely chopped fresh parsley
125ml/4 fl oz crème fraîche
2 garlic cloves

Preparation time:
30 minutes
Cooking time:
1 hour
Nutritional value:
Analysis per serving, approx:
• 3600kJ/860kcal
• 28g protein
• 61g fat
• 34g carbohydrate

Peel and thinly slice the potatoes. • Peel and thinly slice the onions and push out into rings. • Melt half the lard in a gratin dish. Arrange the potato slices and onion rings in layers over the base, seasoning each layer with salt and pepper and sprinkling over the thyme. • Pour in the meat stock, cover the dish with aluminium foil and bake in a preheated oven at 200°C/400°F/gas mark 6 for 40 minutes. • Rinse the pork chops and pat dry. Make a number of cuts across the fatty rind. Melt the remaining lard, and fry the chops over a high heat for 2 minutes on each side. Season to taste with salt and pepper. • Stir the parsley into the crème fraîche. Crush the garlic, and stir into the crème fraîche. Season to taste with salt and pepper. • Remove the gratin dish from the oven. Place the chops on top of the potato and onions, pour over the crème fraîche mixture and bake for a further 20 minutes until the meat is tender. • Serve with a green salad.

42

Escalope of Pork Milanese

50g/2oz Emmenthal cheese, grated
½ tsp dried oregano
75g/3oz breadcrumbs
Salt and freshly ground white pepper
2 eggs
4 tbsps flour
4 x 150g/5oz thin pork escalopes
40g/1½oz butter
5 tbsps oil
1 lemon, thinly sliced

Preparation time:
20 minutes
Nutritional value:
Analysis per serving, approx:
• 2600kJ/620kcal
• 45g protein
• 38g fat
• 22g carbohydrate

Mix together the cheese, oregano, breadcrumbs and ½ tsp pepper. • Beat the eggs. Sift the flour onto a plate. • Rinse the pork, pat dry and sprinkle with salt. • Heat the butter and oil. • Dip the pork first in the flour, then in the beaten eggs and allow any excess to drip off. Finally dip the pork in the cheese and breadcrumb mixture. • Fry the pork over a medium heat for 4–5 minutes on each side. • Transfer to four individual plates and garnish with the lemon slices.

Escalope of Pork in Paprika Cream Sauce

3 small red peppers
1 onion
2 garlic cloves
4 x 150g/5oz pork escalopes
25g/1oz butter
1 tbsp oil
Salt and freshly ground black pepper
1 tbsp sweet paprika
1 tsp hot paprika
250ml/8 fl oz water
200ml/6 fl oz single cream

Preparation time:
50 minutes
Nutritional value:
Analysis per serving, approx:
• 2100kJ/500kcal
• 34g protein
• 35g fat
• 10g carbohydrate

Halve, seed, rinse and dry the peppers. Cut into matchstick strips. • Peel and chop the onion and garlic. • Rinse the pork escalopes and pat dry. • Heat the butter and oil, and fry the pork over a high heat for 4 minutes on each side. Season to taste with salt and pepper, transfer to a dish and keep warm. • Mix the onion and garlic with two thirds of the pepper strips, and gently fry in the same pan for 15 minutes. Add the sweet paprika and hot paprika, and season to taste with salt and pepper. Add the water and bring to the boil. Carefully transfer the mixture to a food processor or blender and work to form a purée. • Return the purée to the frying pan. Stir in the cream and the remaining pepper strips. • Return the pork escalopes and the meat juices to the pan to heat through. • Transfer to four individual plates and serve with tagliatelle.

Grilled Spare Ribs

4 tbsps clear honey
4 tbsps tomato purée
1 tbsp soy sauce
4 garlic cloves
Pinch of hot paprika
Salt and freshly ground black
pepper
2kg/4½lbs spare ribs (ask your
butcher to cut into portions)
2 tbsps sunflower oil

Marinating time:
1 hour
Preparation time:
15 minutes
Cooking time:
40 minutes
Nutritional value:
Analysis per serving, approx:
• 3900kJ/930kcal
• 39g protein
• 82g fat
• 10g carbohydrate

Gently heat the honey in a small saucepan until runny. • Remove from the heat, and stir in the tomato purée and soy sauce. Peel and crush the garlic. Add the garlic and paprika to the honey mixture, and season to taste with salt and pepper. • Rinse and drain the ribs. Rub in a little salt and pepper. Brush the honey sauce over the ribs and wrap them in aluminium foil. Set aside in the refrigerator to marinate for 1 hour. • Brush the grill rack with oil. Cook the ribs under a preheated grill for 30–40 minutes, turning frequently, until cooked through and tender. • Serve with fresh bread and cucumber salad.

Our tip: Butchers do not always have spare ribs instantly available, so it is advisable to order a day in advance.

Turkish-style Shashlik

600g/1lb 6oz lean, tender lamb
5 tbsps olive oil
1 tbsp finely chopped fresh parsley
1 tbsp finely chopped fresh mint
Freshly ground black pepper
150g/5oz smoked streaky bacon, rinded

Marinate for 4 hours
Preparation time:
25 minutes
Nutritional value:
Analysis per serving, approx:
• 2800kJ/670kcal
• 31g protein
• 61g fat
• 1g carbohydrate

Rinse the lamb and pat dry. Trim off any fat or skin and cut into cubes about 4 x 1cm/1½ x ½inches. Place the meat in a shallow dish. • Mix together the oil, parsley and mint, and season to taste with pepper. Pour the oil and herb mixture over the meat, cover and leave in the refrigerator to marinate for 4 hours. • Cut the bacon into strips. Drain the lamb. Thread the lamb cubes and bacon alternately onto four metal skewers. • Place the kebabs in a large grill pan, and cook under a preheated grill for 12-15 minutes, turning frequently, until brown. Brush frequently with the marinade. • Serve with pilau rice and a tomato salad.

Our tip: *An even tastier version of shashlik includes onion segments and slices of pepper threaded on the skewers between the pieces of meat.*

Pork Fillet Kebabs with Prunes

250g/8oz stoned prunes
375ml/14 fl oz dry white wine
1 tsp white peppercorns
1 clove
1 tsp coriander seeds
1 small chilli
Salt and freshly ground black pepper
500g/1lb 2oz pork fillet
1 tsp paprika
40g/1½oz butter

Preparation time:
1¼ hours
Nutritional value:
Analysis per serving, approx:
• 2100kJ/500kcal
• 25g protein
• 20g fat
• 45g carbohydrate

Place the prunes, wine, peppercorns, clove, coriander seeds, chilli and a little salt in a pan, bring to the boil and simmer for 10 minutes. Remove from the heat and set aside for 30 minutes. • Rinse the pork and pat dry. Cut into bite-sized chunks. Rub with salt, pepper and paprika. • Drain the prunes. Thread the prunes and pork alternately onto metal skewers. • Melt the butter in a large frying pan, and fry the kebabs for 15-20 minutes, turning frequently, until brown. • Serve with rice and a curry and butter sauce.

Sweet-and-sour Pork

500g/1lb 2oz pork escalopes
1 tbsp soy sauce
4 spring onions
2 garlic cloves
1 green pepper
3 medium tomatoes
2 slices fresh pineapple
250g/8oz mushrooms
1 tbsp arrowroot
4 tbsps sunflower oil
Salt
Pinch of cayenne pepper
1 tbsp sugar
2 tbsps white wine vinegar
2 tbsps pineapple juice
1 tbsp rice wine or sherry

Preparation time:
45 minutes
Nutritional value:
Analysis per serving, approx:
• 1700kJ/400kcal
• 31g protein
• 20g fat
• 26g carbohydrate

Rinse the pork and pat dry. Cut it into strips. Mix it with the soy sauce, cover and leave to marinate. • Rinse the spring onions and cut into rings. Peel and chop the garlic. Halve, seed, wash and chop the pepper. Skin and chop the tomatoes. • Peel, core and chop the pineapple slices. Rinse and thinly slice the mushrooms. • Sprinkle the arrowroot over the pork and mix well. Heat the oil, and fry the pork until brown. Season to taste with salt and cayenne pepper. Remove from the pan and keep warm. • Fry the spring onions, garlic and mushrooms in the same pan. Add the tomatoes, pepper and pineapple, and cook for a further 2 minutes. • Mix together the sugar, vinegar, pineapple juice and rice wine or sherry. Add the vinegar mixture to the pan, and bring to the boil. • Mix together the pork and vegetables and serve immediately.

Indonesian-style Pork

400g/14oz pork fillet
2 carrots
150g/5oz Savoy cabbage
2 spring onions
100g/4oz soya bean sprouts
3 tbsps vegetable oil
150g/5oz can sliced bamboo
shoots, drained
2 tbsps soy sauce
Pinch of sambal
Salt and freshly ground white
pepper
½ tsp cornflour
2 tbsps water

Preparation time:
40 minutes
Nutritional value:
Analysis per serving, approx:
• 1300kJ/310kcal
• 24g protein
• 17g fat
• 15g carbohydrate

Trim the pork, rinse and pat dry. Cut it into thin strips. • Peel the carrots and cut into matchstick strips. Rinse the cabbage, shake dry and shred. Trim and rinse the onions, and cut into rings. • Rinse the bean sprouts and drain. • Heat half the oil in a large frying pan, and fry the meat in batches until brown. Set aside and keep warm. • Add the remaining oil to the pan, and stir-fry the bamboo shoots for 2 minutes. Add the carrot, and stir-fry for 2 minutes. Add the cabbage, and stir-fry for 1 minute. Add the onions, and stir-fry for 1 minute. Add the bean sprouts and stir-fry for 1 minute. Cook the vegetables, stirring constantly, until tender but still firm to the bite. Return the meat to the pan. Add the soy sauce and sambal, and season to taste with salt and pepper. Heat through. • Mix the cornflour with the water to make a paste. Add to the pan and stir until thickened. • Transfer to a serving dish and serve with rice.

Our tip: *A pinch of chilli powder and a dash of lime juice may be substituted for sambal, but the flavour will not be authentic.*

Veal Roulade with Mushrooms

4 x 100g/4oz veal escalopes
100g/4oz streaky bacon,
rinded
2 onions
500g/1lb 2oz mushrooms
8 sage leaves
2 tbsps sunflower oil
Salt and freshly ground white
pepper
125ml/4 fl oz dry white wine
250ml/8 fl oz chicken stock
3 tbsps crème fraîche
1 tsp cornflour
Pinch of sweet paprika

Preparation time:
35 minutes
Cooking time:
45 minutes
Nutritional value:
Analysis per serving, approx:
• 1800kJ/430kcal
• 28g protein
• 29g fat
• 11g carbohydrate

Rinse the escalopes and pat dry. • Dice the bacon.

Peel and chop the onions. Thinly slice half the mushrooms. • Fry the bacon in a dry pan over a low heat until the fat runs. Add half the onion, and fry until soft. Add the sliced mushrooms, and fry for 5 minutes. Divide the mixture between the escalopes, and top each with 2 sage leaves. Roll up firmly, and secure with trussing thread. • Heat the oil, and fry the remaining onions. Add the rolls, and fry over a high heat, turning to brown all over. Season with salt and pepper. Add the wine and stock, cover and simmer for 30 minutes. • Halve the remaining mushrooms, add to the pan and cook for 10 minutes. • Transfer the roulades to a serving dish, remove the thread and keep warm. • Boil the cooking liquid. Mix the crème fraîche, cornflour and paprika, stir into the sauce and bring to the boil. • Pour over the roulades. Serve with tagliatelle and grilled tomatoes.

Pork Roulade with Cheese

4 x 150g/5oz pork escalopes
4 tbsps torn fresh basil leaves
150g/5oz mascarpone cheese
Salt and freshly ground white
pepper
1 tsp lemon juice
500g/1lb 2oz tomatoes
200g/7oz mozzarella cheese
2 garlic cloves
4 thin slices Parma ham
3 tbsps olive oil
250ml/8 fl oz hot chicken
stock
1 tsp cornflour
1 tbsp tomato purée

Preparation time:
1 hour
Nutritional value:
Analysis per serving, approx:
• 2600kJ/620kcal
• 50g protein
• 43g fat
• 7g carbohydrate

R inse the pork and pat dry.
• Stir the basil leaves into
the mascarpone with salt and
pepper to taste and the lemon
juice. • Skin the tomatoes and
cut into strips. Dice the
mozzarella. Peel the garlic and
cut into thin slivers. • Spread
the escalopes with the
mascarpone and top with 1
slice of ham. Divide the
tomatoes, mozzarella cheese
and garlic between the
escalopes. Roll up the pork
firmly, and secure with trussing
thread. Rub a little salt and
pepper into the surface. • Heat
the oil, and fry the roulades,
turning until brown all over.
Add the stock, cover and
simmer for 45 minutes. •
Transfer the roulades to a
serving dish, remove the thread
and keep warm. • Boil the
cooking liquid to reduce
slightly. Mix a little sauce with
the cornflour then stir into the
sauce with the tomato purée.
Cook, stirring, until thickened.
Pour the sauce over the
roulades and serve
immediately.

Diamond Roast Pork

Serves 6:
1 garlic clove
Salt and freshly ground black pepper
½ tsp ground caraway seeds
1.5kg/3½lbs loin of pork with rind
1 large onion
500ml/16 fl oz hot water
1 tsp sunflower oil
8 potatoes
250ml/8 fl oz light ale

Preparation time:
30 minutes
Cooking time:
2 hours
Nutritional value:
Analysis per serving, approx:
• 3500kJ/830kcal
• 46g protein
• 57g fat
• 25g carbohydrate

Peel and chop the garlic, and crush with a little salt. Mix together the crushed garlic, 1 tsp pepper and the caraway seeds, and rub into the meat. • Peel the onion and cut into quarters. Place the onion in a roasting tin and pour over the water. Place the roasting tin on a low shelf in a preheated oven at 200°C/400°F/ gas mark 4. • Brush a roasting rack with the oil, and position the pork on it rind side down. Roast for 1 hour. • Peel and thinly slice the potatoes. • Remove the pork from the oven, and score a diamond pattern in the rind. • Reduce the oven temperature to 180°C/350°F/ gas mark 4. • Place the potatoes in the roasting tin, and return the pork to the roasting rack, rind side up. Cook for a further 40 minutes. • Spoon the beer over the pork rind, and continue cooking for a further 20 minutes, basting the rind with the beer from time to time. • Transfer the pork to a carving dish, and leave to stand for 15 minutes. Carve into slices, and serve with the potatoes, onions and cooking juices. Braised sauerkraut is a delicious accompaniment.

Roast Pork with Apricots

Serves 8:
2kg/4½lbs boneless loin of pork with rind
200g/7oz dried apricots
Salt and freshly ground black pepper
250ml/8 fl oz single cream
Pinch of sugar
2 tsps cornflour
2 tbsps flaked almonds

Preparation time:
30 minutes
Cooking time:
2 hours
Nutritional value:
Analysis per serving, approx:
• 3600kJ/860kcal
• 45g protein
• 68g fat
• 20g carbohydrate

Wash the pork and pat dry. Pierce a hole in the middle of one end. Thrust the handle of a wooden spoon into the hole, pushing it the length of the joint. Rotate the handle to widen the hole. • Wash the apricots, and stuff them into the hole. • Make diagonal cuts in the pork rind, and rub in a little salt and pepper. • Place the meat in a roasting tin and cook in a preheated oven at 200°C/400°F/gas mark 6 for 2 hours. Every 25 minutes, add a little hot water to the pan and spoon some over the meat. • Transfer the pork to a serving dish, and keep warm. • Set the roasting tin over a low heat. Add a little hot water, and scrape the base of the tin with a wooden spatula to deglaze. Stir in the cream and sugar. Mix the cornflour with a little water to make a smooth paste. Add the paste to the sauce, and cook, stirring, until thickened. Stir in the flaked almonds. • Serve the roast pork with the sauce, and Brussels sprouts and potatoes.

Stuffed Belly of Pork

Serves 8:
1 onion
40g/1½oz lard
300g/10oz Savoy cabbage
Salt and freshly ground black pepper
½ tsp ground caraway seeds
1 tbsp French mustard
200g/7oz coarse liver sausage
1.2kg/2¾lbs belly of pork
2 bouquets garnis
375ml/14 fl oz beef stock

Preparation time:
1 hour
Cooking time:
1½ hours
Nutritional value:
Analysis per serving, approx:
• 3400kJ/800kcal
• 45g protein
• 75g fat
• 7g carbohydrate

Peel and finely chop the onion. Melt half the lard, and fry the onion until soft. • Wash and shred the cabbage. Add to the pan, and fry for about 15 minutes. Season to taste with salt and pepper, and mix in half the caraway seeds, and the mustard and liver sausage. • Rub the meat with a little salt and pepper. Sprinkle over the remaining caraway seeds, and spread the cabbage mixture over the pork, leaving a margin of about 2cm/1inch. • Roll up the meat, Swiss roll fashion, starting from the thick end, and secure with trussing thread. • Heat the remaining lard in a roasting tin, and brown the rolled pork well on all sides. • Pour the stock over the pork, add the bouquets garnis, and cook in a preheated oven at 240°C/475°F/gas mark 9 for 20 minutes. • Cover the joint, lower the temperature to 180°C/350°F/gas mark 4 and cook for a further 1 hour. • Transfer the pork to a carving dish and keep warm. Discard the bouquets garnis, and strain the cooking juices. Carve the pork into slices, and arrange on a serving dish. Hand the sauce separately.

Wild Rabbit in Soured Cream

*1 wild rabbit (about
1kg/2¼lbs)
Salt and freshly ground black
pepper
500ml/16 fl oz soured cream
50g/2oz brown breadcrumbs
1 tbsp Dijon mustard
1 tsp finely chopped fresh
thyme
1 tsp crushed juniper berries
50g/2oz butter
250ml/8 fl oz dry rosé wine*

Marinate for 24 hours
Preparation time:
20 minutes
Cooking time:
1 hour
Nutritional value:
Analysis per serving, approx:
• 2940kJ/700kcal
• 76g protein
• 41g fat
• 18g carbohydrate

Cut the rabbit into 8 pieces. Rub in a little pepper. Place the rabbit pieces in a bowl, and spoon over the soured cream. Cover and leave to marinate for 24 hours in the refrigerator. • Remove the rabbit pieces from the marinade, gently scraping off the soured cream. Reserve the soured cream. • Mix together the breadcrumbs, mustard, thyme and juniper berries, and season to taste with salt and pepper. Coat the rabbit portions with the mixture. • Place the rabbit in a roasting tin, and cover with the reserved soured cream. Dot with half the butter. Add the wine. • Roast the rabbit in a preheated oven at 220° C/425° F/gas mark 7 for 30 minutes, basting every 10 minutes. • Turn the rabbit pieces over and dot with the remaining butter. Cook for a 30 minutes. • Transfer the rabbit to a serving dish and keep warm. Add a little hot water to the roasting tin, and warm through over a low heat, scraping the base of the tin to deglaze. Hand the sauce separately.

57

Rabbit with Red Peppers

Serves 8:
2 x 1.4kg/3lbs rabbits
Salt and freshly ground black pepper
8 tbsps olive oil
Small piece dried chilli
750g/1lb 10oz tomatoes
6 red peppers
6 large onions
5 garlic cloves
150g/5oz stoned black olives
250ml/8 fl oz dry red wine

Preparation time:
50 minutes
Cooking time:
45 minutes
Nutritional value:
Analysis per serving, approx:
• 3300kJ/790kcal
• 77g protein
• 42g fat
• 21g carbohydrate

Cut the rabbit into 8 portions or ask the butcher to do this for you. • Rinse and pat dry. Rub in a little salt and pepper. • Heat half the oil in a large frying pan, add the chilli and fry the rabbit pieces until brown and crisp on all sides. • Discard the chilli, and set the rabbit pieces aside. • Skin and quarter the tomatoes. Halve, seed and wash the peppers. Pat dry, and cut into wide strips. Peel and quarter the onions. Peel and finely chop the garlic. Halve the olives. • Heat half the remaining oil, and fry the onions and garlic until soft. Add the peppers, olives and tomatoes, and gently fry for 1–2 minutes. Add the red wine. Season to taste with salt and pepper. • Lightly brush a

roasting tin with the remaining olive oil. • Place the vegetables in the tin, add the rabbit and roast in a preheated oven at 200°C/400°F/gas mark 6 for 45 minutes. • From time to time, check the amount of liquid in the roasting tin, and add a little more wine if the vegetables are drying out. • Transfer the rabbit and vegetables, together with the cooking juices, to a large serving dish, and serve immediately. • Serve with crusty bread and the same red wine as that used for the sauce.

Our tip: The spiciness of this dish depends on the chilli. People who enjoy hot dishes may wish to use a whole chilli. However, it is not advisable to overdo the amount of chilli, as it can easily dominate the other flavours.
Those who do not like hot spices can omit the chilli and season with cayenne pepper instead.

Spicy Game Stew

1kg/2¼lbs shoulder of venison
2 onions
6 cloves
1 leek
1 carrot
6 tbsps sunflower oil
500ml/16 fl oz red wine
3 tbsps red wine vinegar
1 thick slice of lemon
2 bay leaves
5 black peppercorns
Salt and freshly ground pepper
2 tbsps flour
1 tsp sugar
125ml/4 fl oz hot beef stock
1 tbsp cranberry jelly

Preparation time:
40 minutes
Marinate for 24 hours
Cooking time:
1½ hours
Nutritional value:
Analysis per serving, approx:
• 2200kJ/520kcal
• 56 g protein
• 16 g fat
• 17 g carbohydrate

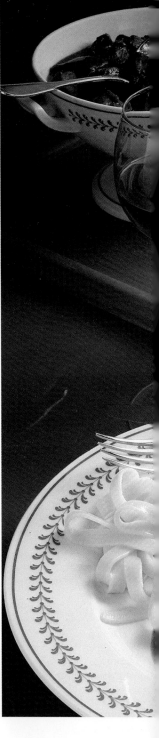

Rinse the meat and pat dry. • Peel 1 of the onions and stud it with 3 cloves. • Wash and slice the leek. Peel and slice the carrot. • Heat 1 tbsp of the oil, and fry the leek and carrot for 5 minutes. • Reserve 4 tbsps of the wine. Mix the remaining wine, the vinegar, studded onion, leek and carrot, lemon slice, 1 bay leaf and peppercorns. Pour over the venison, cover and marinate for 24 hours in a cool place. Stir frequently. • Drain the venison. Strain and reserve the marinade. • Heat 3 tbsps of the remaining oil, and fry the meat for 15 minutes, stirring frequently. Season with salt and pepper. • Add the reserved marinade, bring to the boil and simmer for 1 hour. • Remove the venison from the pan and reserve 375ml/14 fl oz of the cooking liquid. Bone and cube the meat. • Heat the remaining oil, add the flour and sugar and cook, stirring, for 1-2 minutes until golden brown. Gradually stir in the stock and cooking liquid. Peel the remaining onion and stud with the

60

remaining cloves. Add the
onion and remaining bay leaf
to the pan, and simmer for 15
minutes. • Remove and discard
the onion and bay leaf. Stir in
the remaining red wine and
cranberry jelly, and heat
through. • Serve with pasta.

61

Medallions of Venison with Fruit

300g/10oz fresh pineapple
1 large orange
1 large tart apple
1 banana
2 tbsps Cointreau
2 tbsps lemon juice
600g/1lb 6oz venison fillet
4 slices white bread about
1½cm/¾inch thick
50g/2oz butter
Salt and freshly ground white
pepper

Preparation time:
45 minutes
Nutritional value:
Analysis per serving, approx:
• 2000kJ/480kcal
• 37g protein
• 15g fat
• 44g carbohydrate

Peel and core the pineapple, and dice the flesh. Peel the orange and remove the pith. Cut the flesh into pieces. Peel and core the apple and cut into slices. Peel and slice the banana. • Mix together the Cointreau and lemon juice and sprinkle over the fruit. Cover and leave to stand. • Rinse the venison, pat dry and cut off any skin. Cut the fillet into four equal slices and press flat with the heel of the hand. • Cut the slices of bread to the same shape as the medallions. • Melt 25g/1oz of the butter, and fry the bread on both sides until golden brown. Remove from the heat and keep warm. • Melt the remaining butter, and fry the venison for 3 minutes on each side. The inner flesh should be a pale pink colour. Season to taste with salt and pepper. • Arrange the fried bread on a serving plate and top with the medallions. Pour over the butter and meat juices and serve with the fresh fruit.

Venison Escalopes Flambé

4 x 150g/5oz venison
escalopes
2 tbsps walnut oil
1 tsp dried rosemary
2 kiwi fruit
15g/½oz butter
4 walnuts, shelled
Salt and freshly ground white
pepper
2 tbsps brandy

Marinate for 2 hours
Preparation time:
30 minutes
Nutritional value:
Analysis per serving, approx:
• 1200kJ/290kcal
• 34g protein
• 11g fat
• 7g carbohydrate

Rinse the venison, pat dry and cut off any skin. Rub in the walnut oil, and sprinkle over the rosemary. Place the meat slices one on top of the other, wrap in aluminium foil and marinate for 2 hours in the refrigerator. • Peel the kiwi fruit and cut into slices. Melt the butter over a low heat, add the kiwi fruit and warm through. Do not brown. • Roughly chop the walnuts. • Heat a heavy-based frying pan, and fry the venison over a high heat for 2–3 minutes on each side. Season to taste with salt and pepper, and transfer to a flameproof serving dish. • Sprinkle over the chopped walnuts and arrange the kiwi slices on top. • Warm the brandy in a ladle over a flame. Pour the warm brandy over the venison, ignite and serve flaming. • Potato croquettes make a good accompaniment.

Index